unravel
MY HEALING HEART

GINA KANTZAS

Copyright © 2023 Gina Kantzas

All rights reserved. No part of this book may be reproduced by any mechanical, photographic, or electronic process, or in the form of a phonographic recording, nor may it be stored in a retrieval system, transmitted, or otherwise be copied for public or private use—other than for 'fair use' as brief quotations embodied in articles and reviews—without prior written permission of the publisher.

Published in Australia

Printed in Australia

First Edition

ISBN: 978-0-6459802-0-2

Cover and Interior Design: Kelly Exeter

To my beloved dad.

Anyone can tell a story, but not everyone has listeners.

Anyone can love but not everyone can make others feel loved.

contents

INTRODUCTION 7

Just, begin 11

What shall I do today? 12

Before the Sun 14

Begin Again 16

Keep Your Body Moving 18

On the Threshold.. 20

What I know now, I always knew 22

Compassion arises from curiosity 24

I do not live a life 26

The pieces of me 28

Forgiveness 30

I will 32

My Love 34

I called my Mum 36

Mama Bear 38

My Brother 40

Father's Day 42

Whispers 44

Tenderness	46
Stillness Speaks	48
Awaken	50
Sitting Pretty	52
Sad and Hopeful	54
The magic of now	56
Here I am	58
I am. You are.	60
I will never forget you	62
Sun, Sand and Sadness	64
The Drop in the Ocean	66
Manifestation	68
The Golden Rays	70
Love you dearly	72
Love on the spectrum	74
Witness me	76
Surrender	78
Remember	80
THANK YOU	83

introduction

2020 was a time of community-wide fear, control and contraction. Initially, I felt relieved to rest from the race I was running, the race many of us were. I relaxed into the slow mornings with nowhere to go and no one to see. No deadlines, no expectations and no obligations. My alone time became my free time. Time to meditate, time to write and time to connect with myself.

As the days turned to weeks, the connection to my thoughts, body and my heart felt deeper. But soon, this alone time became my lonely time. When the weeks turned to months, the scary signs of sadness began catching up with me. The overwhelming feeling of separation set in. My nervous system gripped my body and my mind imprisoned my thoughts of judgement and hopelessness.

Amongst this internal thunder, my inner voice arose in a whisper. The more I noticed it, the louder it became. My intuition beckoned me to the peacefulness found in self-compassion. There were many nudges to write, and at times it felt like I was downloading from a stream. The words would flow. And time would stop.

Reconnecting with my soul after years of continual attempts to hide from its voice gave rise to challenges when my world, the world of work and family, opened back up and closed back down again on repeat for the next couple of years. Each time I faced another crisis during my evolution, I remembered these poems. They felt validating and empowering.

They felt like love notes.

The more I changed, the more I wanted to change.

The more I paused, the more I learned that loneliness is only a breath away. We can all feel it, at any time. It's the swallowing of the tears meant to wash the fears. It's the withdrawing of your hand when unworthiness takes hold.

Expressing my feelings in written form carried me through some of the most difficult times I have faced as a mother, daughter, and girlfriend. The more I wrote, the more I met my true self.

Sometimes I read the words as healing, and sometimes I read the words as inspiration. I hope you read the words with your heart and know that you are not alone. Because this is my truth – when I witness myself, I matter, and when I matter, so do you.

This book chronicles my evolution through my devotion. And it is my dedication to the ones like me who want to be free.

Love, Gina.

just, begin

Start where you are. And first you are home.

Start when you can. And first you feel the spark.

Start what you know. And first hear your voice.

There's no time for judgement. Time isn't a factor.

There's no space for doubt. Your space
is for compassion.

Right or wrong is an illusion. Flow is the gateway.

Words can be your nemesis. Surrender to the flow.

Honour the truth they tell. And thank them for
the challenge they reveal.

Feel the hurt, the frustration, the unworthiness.

Trust. There is timing in your words.

Start. Write now and you will be revealed.

Liberation, love and lightness will rise.

what shall I do today?

What shall I do today?
Who will I see?

What shall I feel today?
Who will stand by me?

What will I hear today?
Who will I touch?

How can I reach out today?
Will I see from above?

Can I feel the sun today through the rain?
Will my smile be enough when there's pain?

Can I be still today, and be free?

Hold on tight then let it go
Breathe in all that you know

Stand up tall and feel your wings
Pause again and your heart will sing

Sway with the trees, don't choose just one
Shine your light alongside the sun

Connect and weave and dissolve again
Love the waves within your heart, my friend

Inside again and there will be light
Quiet again and there will be peace

Find your calm and you will see
All you need today is to rest with me

Just be

before the sun

Before the sun
Before the day
Before you seek
to find your way

Drop into your body
where feelings are simmering
Drop into your knowing
that stirs your soul

The truth will be warm
The truth will be light
Your truth will be flowing
It's in your heart

Tap into this feeling
of loose and carefree
Tap into this energy
of what is meant to be

Trust you have found it
Trust for this day
Trust when it speaks to you
when it shows you the way

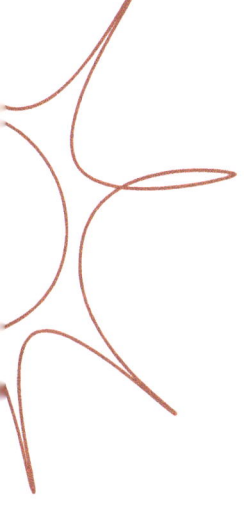

There's no place for the how
There's no place for the why
Don't ask for the when
just give it a try

Try with commitment
that you cannot fail
Try with belief
that you can fly

There's a knowing within you
There's a guide just for you
There's experience to lean on
And there's a joy to find

Reach for the love
that is all you really know
Reach for the intention
of compassion and understanding

Connect with yourself
Say hello to your presence
Touch the earth
Open up to the sky

Sense your being
then radiate from there
And feel the love
Before you start your day

begin again

As I learn and relearn to communicate
from my soul, I will share with you

As I practice expressing from my spirit,
I will share with you

As I begin again, and cradle my creativity,
I will share with you

You are pieces of me. You are visions of me.
You are love I receive.

I will stumble and fall and feel for guidance

I will pray for the light and hold out my hand

I will see you in your glory and
I will feel you in your pain

Be still and step forward

Receive and smile

Share and glow

Let's soften into our unified energy and
rise in our personal power

I share me with you

I sink into us

We begin again

keep your body moving

Keep your body moving

Keep your energy flowing

Keep your wonder at the forefront

Keep your arms open

Keep your eyes wide

Keep your smile brimming

Keep your mind fluid

Keep your shoulders soft

Keep your breath quiet

Keep your voice humming

Keep your hands warm

Keep your feet forward

Keep your chest down

Keep your body swaying

Keep feeling all around

Keep still, over and over

Touch the earth beneath you

Gaze at the sky above

Feel you are protected

And receive infinite love

on the threshold

Within my heart I grieve and grieve

Within my heart I cannot see

The love that's there, that's been all along

The love that pulses, through my wilful song

Within my heart, I ask the questions

What is right and what is fair?

What should I do?

And what do I dare?

On the threshold

I stand and fear

But in my soul

all is clear

what I know now, I always knew

The depth of simplicity can feel endless

So why do we suppress our instincts?
Why do we ignore our intuition?
Why do we stay in our head?

The truth is deeper, wider, higher

Be yourself and you will inspire
Know yourself and you will be loved
Express yourself and you will know kindness

Your self is an observer
Your self is a creator
Your self is boundless love

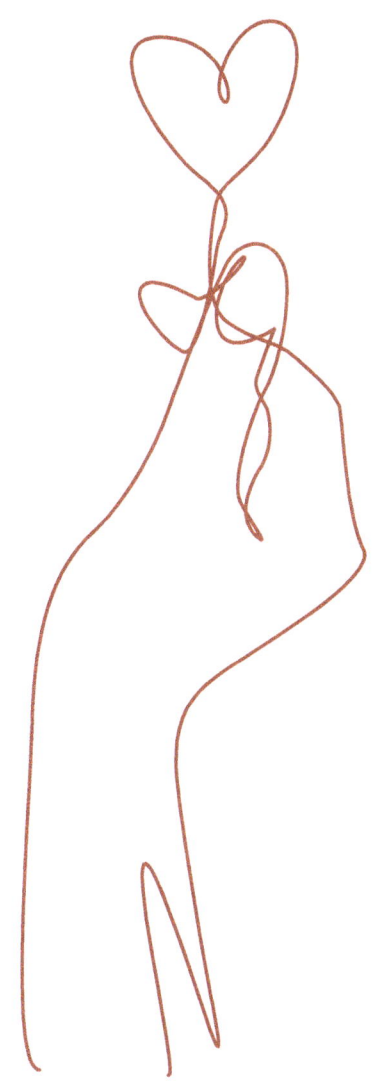

compassion arises from curiosity

Being curious opens up the feelings of
wonder and newness

It creates a recurring fresh start.

Observe without judgement and expectation and
the experience will unfold more effortlessly

Reacting is powerlessness

Curiosity releases the pressure

Drop control and see clearer by listening and feeling

Competitiveness can separate you from who you are

Compassion witnesses the sameness
you have with another

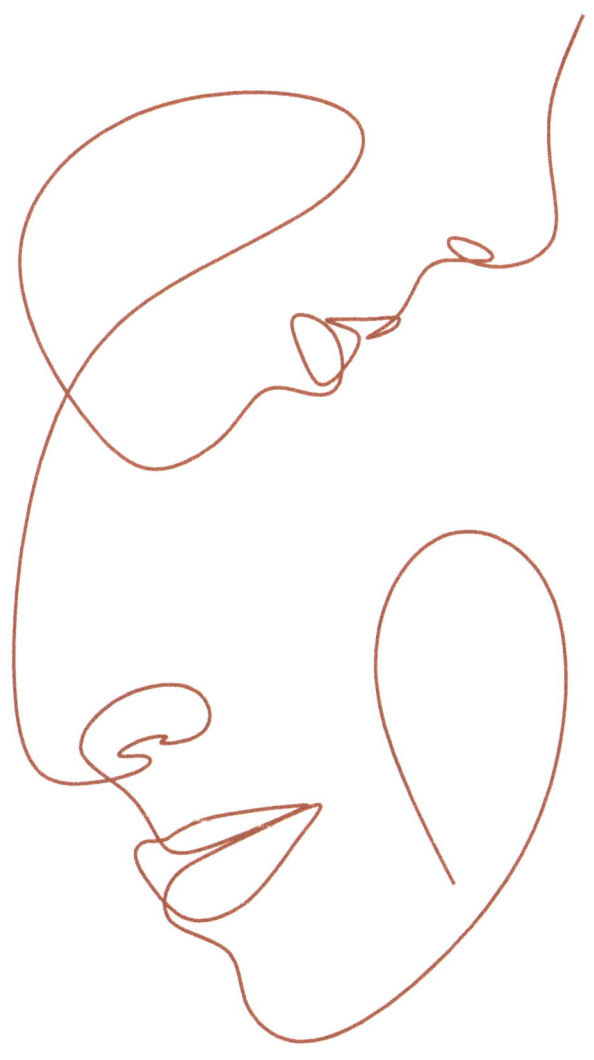

I do not live a life

I do not live a life
Life lives through me

I do not control a life
Life offers colours for me

I do not wish upon a star
I dive into the infinite within

I do not navigate the seas
I drift to many shores

I do not cultivate the fields
I cherish the soil and the seeds

I do not prepare for rain
I accept new beginnings as they arise

I do not shelter from thunder
I smile as two worlds collide

I am but a morsel of life
Yet I can fill and be filled

For I am an energy source
I am one and I am of the same

I can create the day
And I can feel the way

As the life force inside of me
is the life we all can see

the pieces of me

The pieces of me are not here and now
The pieces of me are roaming around
I grasp and I sigh
I am longing and I cry

The pieces of me shoot across and fall behind
The pieces of me light up the sky
I get lost in my gaze
I feel weary in time

The pieces of me are floating on by
The pieces of me don't know space and time
I stumble and rest
I resign and I pray

The pieces of me are not where they should be
The pieces of me are not here with me
They're moving and sensing
They're learning and connecting

The pieces of me float and they buzz
The pieces of me attract and repel
They're far and they're near
They're creating new worlds without any fear

The pieces of me are calling my name
The pieces of me want to come home

forgiveness

Forgive from your soul
Forgive for your soul

For our capabilities are not unique
And our capacities are the same

Our lessons will all be learned
It's just a matter of time

Forgive the pain and the fear
Let go of the anger because you were near

Release the injustice and the overwhelm
And reignite the flow of good will

Unlock the chambers in your heart
Release the energies that are stuck

Watch the sun transform the heaviness all around
And feel the lightness rain down

The rivers of love will run
And the life force in us will rise

The energies of the world will reunite
When the love created radiates all around

Forgiveness is for you
Forgiveness is for me

As forgiveness opens the door
To harmony and ease

I will

How do I look so my eyes don't see?
How do I listen so my ears don't hear?
How do I learn so my mind doesn't understand?
How do I feel so my heart doesn't break?

I will

Look with the eyes of a stranger
Listen with the ears of a mother
Learn with the mind of a warrior
Love with the heart of a saviour

my love

My love, my heart, my dignity, my sorrow
My pain, my glory, my oversight, my hollow

My smile, my gaze, my gasp, my tear
My longing, my open arms, my wish, my fear

My pride, my wallowing, my rise, my call
My people, my places, my interests, my fall

My ups, my downs, my fooling around
My honesty, my defences, my feeling bound

My seeking, my surrender, my layers, my security
My joy, my judgement, my compassion, my empathy

My pedestal, my voice, my quiet, my vision
My acceptance, my reflection, my porosity,
my momentum

My intricacies, my expansiveness, my intention
My choices, my creation, my attention

My flow, my reason, my expression, my being
My seasons, my giving, my sharing, my seeing

My core, my life, my essence, my feeling

My contrast, my contraction, my contradiction
My love, my everything, fact and fiction

I called my mum

I called my mum and noticed her hunger
I called my mum and sensed her fear

I called my mum and felt her sorrow
I called my mum and touched her regret

I called my mum and heard her ancestors
I called my mum and soothed her loneliness

I called my mum and found forgiveness

I called my mum and held the feelings
I called my mum and she was healing

mama bear

The grief is palpable
The love is on fire
The mind is dizzy
The direction is nowhere

Grief is lonely
Empathy painful
Logic hovers
Breathing out is surrendering

Fear is for acceptance
Shame is for the judgement
Self Pity is the silent cry
The roar is mama bear's

Don't rest or retaliate
Don't run or freeze
Remember and recalibrate
And find your peace

Love from the shadows
Love behind the tears
Love flowing endlessly
Love forever and 24 years

my brother

Your pain is my pain
Your longing is my withholding

Your face has my fear
Your body holds my tears

Your eyes see my faults
Your throat holds my love

Your arms squeeze my blood
Your feet stomp my ground

Your hands hang hopelessly
Your legs tighten mightily

Your heart is throbbing
Your breath is heaving

Your life is waiting
My heart is breaking

father's day

Share your smile when someone is flying
Hold out your hands when someone is falling

Share your experience to encourage
others to keep going
Offer your ear to someone who's overwhelmed

Share your knowledge when you have been there
Create quiet when you have not

Share your good news with others to inspire
Recommend others to uplift them
and their adventures

Share your time with an honest focus
And create a loving energy from where you are

Feeling grateful for this moment
And I give of myself from here

So I am reminded to pay it forward
And keep smiling for one and for all

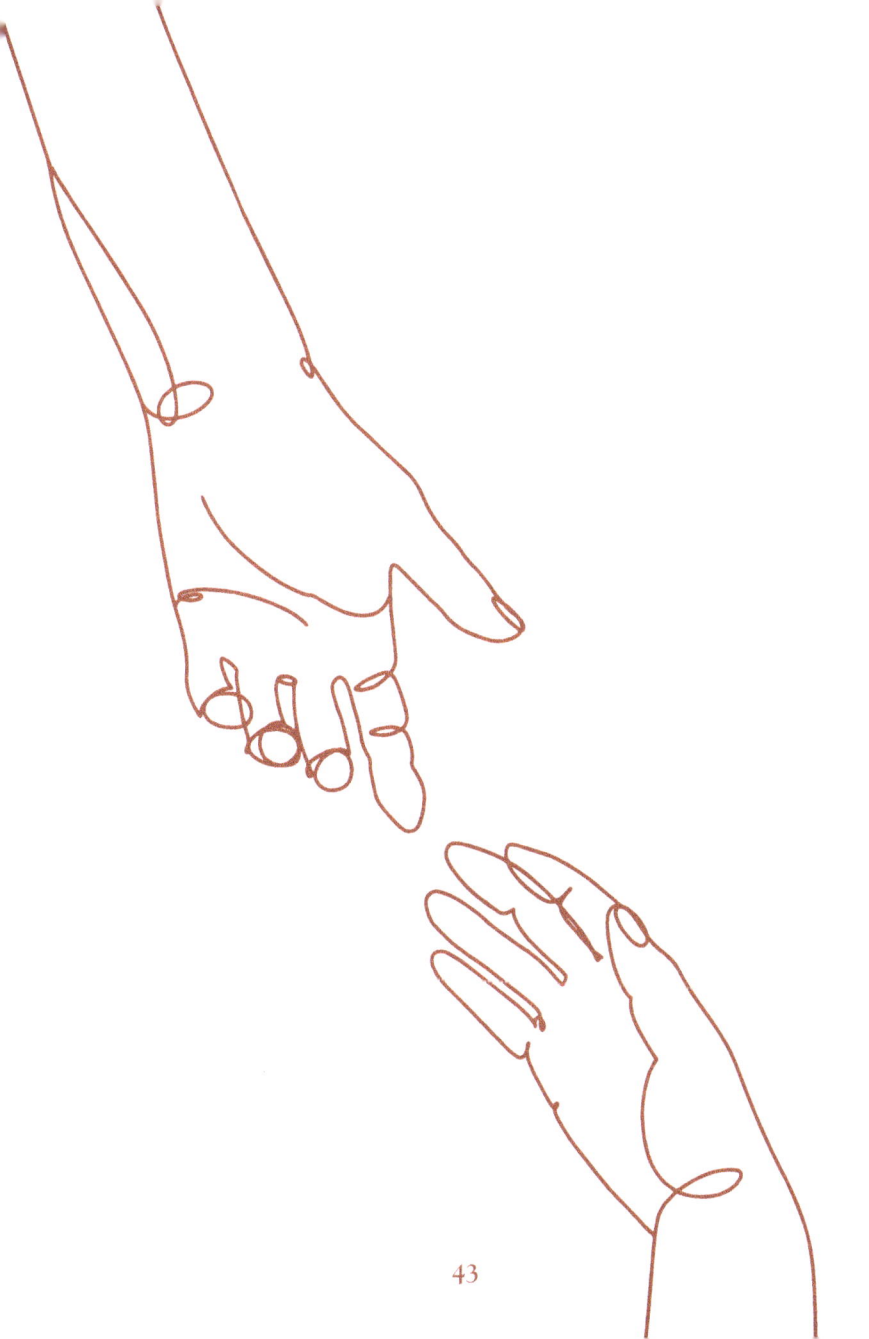

whispers

Gently swirling in the breeze

Quietly floating amongst the clouds

Quickly skipping with the waves

They're lightly tickling my skin

They're softly stroking my mind

It's time to listen with my heart

There are whispers to be felt

There are truths waiting to unfold

There are whispers calling just for you

tenderness

There's such a strength in tenderness
The power of not looking away
The power of looking deeply
The power of recognising the sameness in another

There's such a strength in tenderness
The safety of feeling seen
The safety of being held
The safety of unconditional love

There's such a strength in tenderness
The transformation in stepping into the space
The transformation in accepting what is
The transformation in receiving the love

stillness speaks

Let the tears flow
Let the breath deepen
Let the body sigh
Let the human cry

The human experience can be heavy
Your experience can be slow
Your experience can be burdensome
It can feel like there's nowhere to go

Allow your body to become floppy
Allow your thoughts to wash away
Resign to being cracked open
And breathe in strength to rise another day

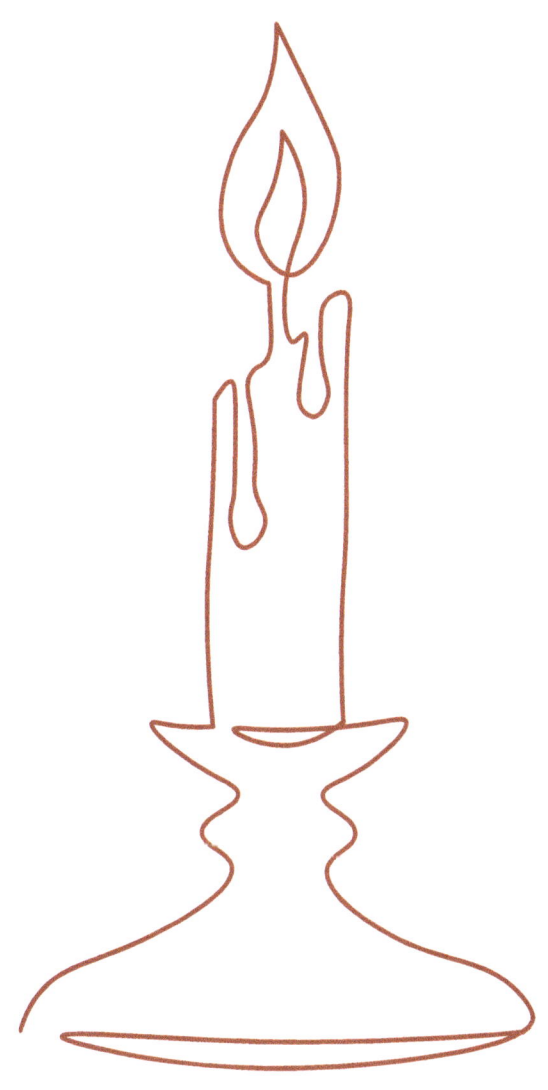

awaken

Rest my beauty
Rest in love
Rest in harmony with what is

Sleep my beauty
Sleep in love
Sleep in peace with what was

Walk my beauty
Walk in love
Walk in joy of what will be

Float my beauty
Float in love
Float above, beside and within

Surrender my beauty
Surrender in love
Surrender into the bliss with me

sitting pretty

Sitting pretty
Standing tall
Waiting graciously
Hoping I don't fall

Standing up
Laying down
Walking slowly
Until I'm found

Thinking loudly
Speaking softly
Heartbeat tender
Feels like forever

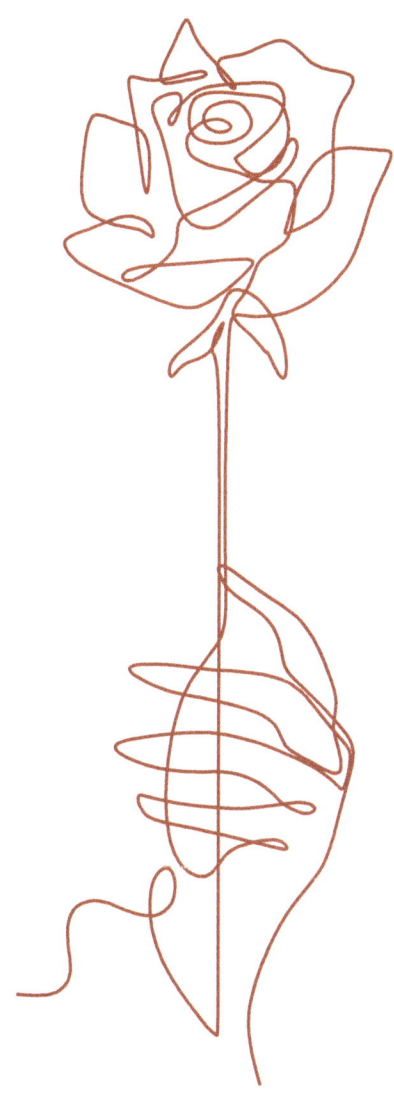

sad and hopeful

Get me out of here
Take me away
I want to get out of here
Why can't I run away?

I could live in the country
I could walk in the fields of green
I could inspire for a living
I could live in a dream

But how would that help?
How would that change a thing?
How would I feel?
What would I bring?

My senses aware
My mind alive
My body weary
My emotions on high

My heart is aching
For adventure and wild
My soul is pleading
For touch and smiles

How long must we wait?
How long mustn't we care?
There's people growing hate
There's people suffering and despair

It's time to breathe in and surrender
It's time to breathe out love and tender
It's time to reach in for peace and reflection
It's time to reach out in hope and connection

the magic of now

A time to remember
How to be
A time to remember
You are no different than me

A time to remember
What is out is also within
A time to remember
There is no lose and no win

A time to remember
There are no shoulds or must do's
A time to remember
There are infinite possibilities for you

A time to remember
Momentum springs from inspiration
A time to remember
Satisfaction arises from fun

A time to remember
To love and let go
A time to remember
To witness life's flow

A time to remember
To cherish awareness
A time to remember
That's all you need to know

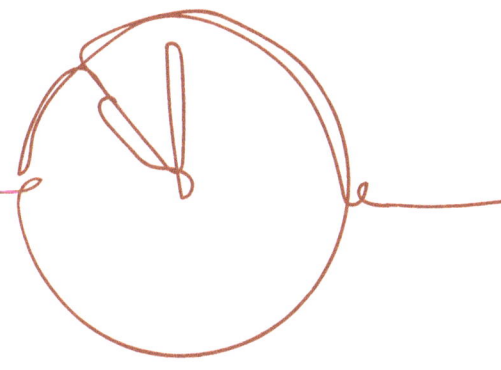

here I am

I release expectations
I shake off frustrations
I feel the melting of triggered sensations

I relax the visions
I tone the words
I leave grasping right alone

I listen with wonder
I ponder with joy
I gaze above and I feel under

Here I am on this earth
Here I am still standing tall
Here I am in all my worth

I am. you are.

Through feeling I heal
Through listening I learn
Through tenderness I transform
Through witnessing I am reborn

My eyes see reflections
of what I feel
My body is the voice
of what I need to heal

I am everything
when I do not deny
And I am everyone
When I sit and cry

But when I smile
I immediately feel lighter
And then I remember
I am Goddess and fighter

I will never forget you

Remembering faith
Embodying trust
Feeling uncomfortable
Becoming unstuck

Transformation with ease
When stillness was not feared
Momentum resisted
When intuition was listened

Freedom found
In depth and simplicity
Peace abounds
From loving implicitly

Goodbye to time and to you
Goodbye to patterns I once knew
Hello truth, I will always love you
Hello my heart, shining anew

sun, sand & sadness

It washes over if you let it
It cleanses within you if you allow it
It invigorates your life force when you let it

Sadness coming up out of nowhere
Sadness rising from the depths of somewhere
Sadness overcoming my awareness

The sun's rays warm my skin
The sand around my feet is cooling
The breeze on my face is refreshing

Here I am
Raw in my honesty
Present with myself
And nowhere to hide

the drop in the ocean

The drop in the ocean
Falls silently down
The drop in the ocean
Calls quietly around
For help from the despair
Which suddenly appears
For a hand in the air
To lift you from the tears

When feeling as the ocean
Gets too much to bear
When feeling as the ocean
Gets you floating through the air
Being grounded feels so far away
And flow feels like swimming upstream

The breath is the grand connector
And the heart is your intimate projector

Let the fire move through you
Burning all that no longer belongs
Let the blood flow again nourishing all that remains
Allow the air out slowly so you move
towards the earth
And the body integrates again for all your worth

manifestation

Sometimes you manifest exactly what you
want and it hurts, a lot.

Your eyes dart as you sense new territory
Your body limp as entanglements have unravelled

The human cries and feels unsafe
The soul sees karma can end in this place

You know there's limitless possibilities for you
You know you don't need to know what to do

You feel the truth sink deeper into your being
You know that trust is what you should be feeling

You know what you need yet think other things
You know right now your heart can't sing

You're releasing the remnants of fear and longing
You're summoning courage to not
reverse the wanting

To stay in this liminal space of
endings and adventure
You engage your faith for another tenure

I will trust, I will trust, I will trust. I pray
I surrender, I surrender, I surrender today

Tomorrow I'll rise harmonious and free
But tonight I'll stay in bed and continue to dream

the golden rays

The golden rays, the golden sky
The love I feel, the love that flys
through oceans and lakes and clouds and thunder
Around fields of green, growing louder and stronger

The golden age, these golden days
They hold the codes to light the way
Connections are creeping and stretching
Karma is longing and people are weeping

Trust is truth, it's stronger than trees
Surrender is the roots to hold the belief
God is everywhere and God is nothing
You are everything, solid and floating

Rejoice this experience, it was meant for you
You are right on time, doing what
you were designed to do

Keep feeling and moving and inching forward
Keep pausing and noticing the love you hoard
Offer yourself, share your wisdom
There's people out there waiting and wishing

love you dearly

Love you dearly
Love you fiercely
Love you quietly
Love you mightily

Love you forever
Love you today
Love you even
when you get in your way

love on the spectrum

Love on the spectrum
Love in all its shades

Love on the continuum
Love in all the ways

Love isn't one thing
Love isn't one feeling

Love is a truth
Love is a healing

Love is ever-evolving
deeper and expanding

Love is a teacher
compassionate & demanding

Love doesn't give up on you
Love sees through your mood

Love is the waves
that carry you through
life's peaks and valleys
back home to you

witness me

Witness me in my joy
Witness me in my sorrow
Witness me in my light
Witness me in my shadow

Witness me when I feel guilty
Witness me as I'm evolving
Witness my accountability
for how I've been loving

surrender

I want to surrender to the sweetness in emotion:

    the joy in your gaze
    the gratitude in your smile
    the safety in your kiss

I want to contain the purity of emotion:

    of that which binds
    the strength of this sweetness
    to carry us with kindness

I want to open to the expression of emotion:

    the fierceness and the protection
    the joy and the honouring
    in the stillness and in the momentum

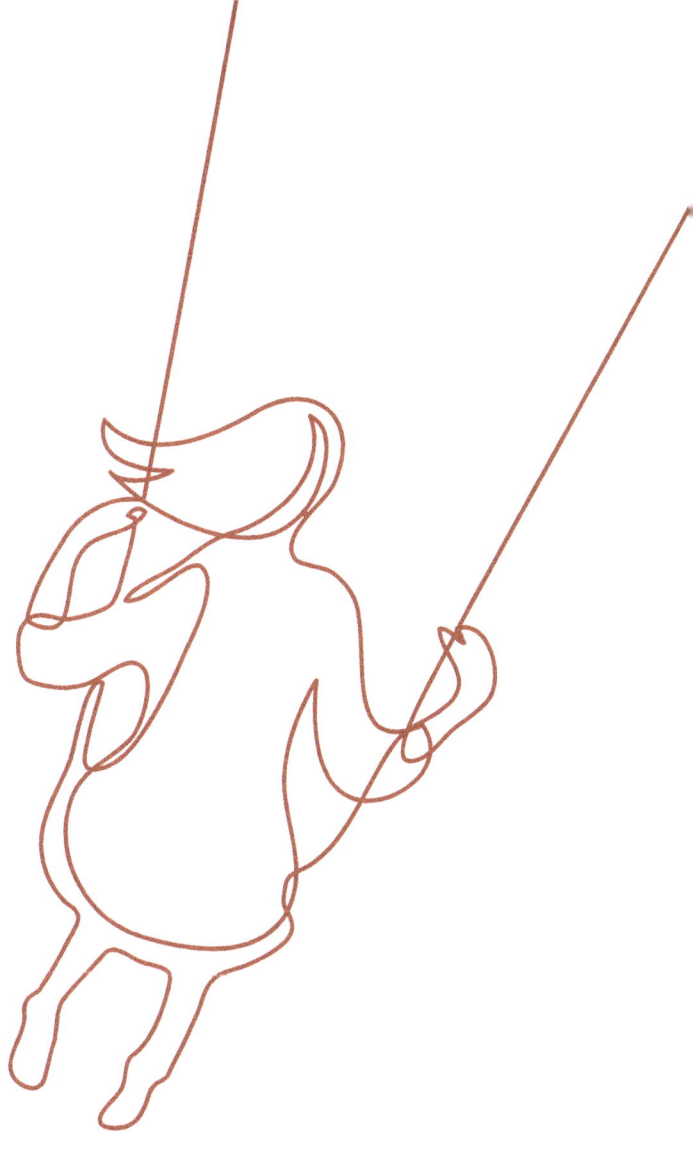

remember

Through feeling I heal
Through listening I learn
Through tenderness I transform
Through witnessing I am reborn

Raw and ripe is my current disposition

Resting in this next transition

♡

thank you

Thank you to my friends and teachers:

Kate Williams for believing in me.

Sonja Bollnow for supporting my soul's expression.

Eryka Stanton for guiding me through a path of self-compassion.

Dr Ricci-Jane Adams for leading me through fear to live life from my intuitive intelligence.

And thank you to my beautiful Koumbari, Maria and Shane Russell, who never fail to check in on me and offer unconditional love.

www.ingramcontent.com/pod-product-compliance
Lightning Source LLC
Chambersburg PA
CBHW042343300426
44109CB00049B/2817